4/16

ANIMAL SAFARI

Red Pandas

by Megan Borgert-Spaniol

BELLWETHER MEDIA · MINNEAPOLIS, MN

Note to Librarians, Teachers, and Parents:

Blastoff! Readers are carefully developed by literacy experts and combine standards-based content with developmentally appropriate text.

Level 1 provides the most support through repetition of high-frequency words, light text, predictable sentence patterns, and strong visual support.

Level 2 offers early readers a bit more challenge through varied simple sentences, increased text load, and less repetition of high-frequency words.

Level 3 advances early-fluent readers toward fluency through increased text and concept load, less reliance on visuals, longer sentences, and more literary language.

Level 4 builds reading stamina by providing more text per page, increased use of punctuation, greater variation in sentence patterns, and increasingly challenging vocabulary.

Level 5 encourages children to move from "learning to read" to "reading to learn" by providing even more text, varied writing styles, and less familiar topics.

Whichever book is right for your reader, Blastoff! Readers are the perfect books to build confidence and encourage a love of reading that will last a lifetime!

This edition first published in 2016 by Bellwether Media, Inc.

No part of this publication may be reproduced in whole or in part without written permission of the publisher. For information regarding permission, write to Bellwether Media, Inc., Attention: Permissions Department, 5357 Penn Avenue South, Minneapolis, MN 55419.

Library of Congress Cataloging-in-Publication Data

Borgert-Spaniol, Megan, 1989- author.
  Red pandas / by Megan Borgert-Spaniol.
    pages cm. – (Blastoff! Readers. Animal Safari)
  Summary: "Developed by literacy experts for students in kindergarten through grade three, this book introduces red pandas to young readers through leveled text and related photos"– Provided by publisher.
  Audience: Ages 5-8
  Audience: K to grade 3
  Includes bibliographical references and index.
  ISBN 978-1-62617-213-5 (hardcover: alk. paper)
  1. Red panda–Juvenile literature. I. Title. II. Series: Blastoff! readers. 1, Animal safari.
  QL737.C214B66 2016
  599.76'3–dc23
                                                                          2015004205

Printed in the United States of America, North Mankato, MN.

Contents

What Are Red Pandas?

Red pandas are **mammals**. They make their homes in **bamboo** forests.

Thick reddish fur covers their bodies. It blends in with the colors of the forest.

Red pandas have long, **ringed** tails. The tails help them **balance** on branches.

8

Red pandas curl
up with their tails
to stay warm.

Food

Red pandas rest in trees during the day. At night they look for food.

Their favorite meal is bamboo. They nibble on bamboo **shoots** and leaves.

They also enjoy fruits, flowers, and acorns. Sometimes they eat bird eggs.

Cubs

A female red panda builds a **den** with plants and twigs. She gives birth to her **cubs** inside.

Mom carries a cub with her mouth. Let's go, cub!

Glossary

balance—to stay steady and not fall

bamboo—a tall plant with a hard, hollow stem

cubs—baby red pandas

den—a place where animals stay safe; red pandas build dens inside tree trunks or under large rocks.

mammals—warm-blooded animals that have backbones and feed their young milk

ringed—striped with bands of color

shoots—plants that are just beginning to grow

To Learn More

AT THE LIBRARY

Marsh, Laura. *Red Pandas*. Washington, D.C.: National Geographic, 2015.

Paul, Ruth. *Red Panda's Candy Apples*. Somerville, Mass.: Candlewick Press, 2014.

Schuetz, Kari. *Giant Pandas*. Minneapolis, Minn.: Bellwether Media, 2012.

ON THE WEB

Learning more about red pandas is as easy as 1, 2, 3.

1. Go to www.factsurfer.com.

2. Enter "red pandas" into the search box.

3. Click the "Surf" button and you will see a list of related Web sites.

With factsurfer.com, finding more information is just a click away.

Index

The images in this book are reproduced through the courtesy of: Hung Chung Chih, front cover; Joe Ravi, p. 5; Lukas Blazek, p. 7; Omarmg, p. 9; digitalpark, p. 11; Olga Bogatyrenko, p. 13; Wildlife Gmbh/ Alamy, pp. 15, 21; PA Bimages, p. 17 (top); Maxim Tupikov, p. 17 (bottom); sabza, p. 17 (bottom left); Africa Studio, p. 17 (bottom center); Miroslav Hlavko, p. 17 (bottom right); David & Micha Sheldon/ Age Fotostock, p. 19.